The EPA

Environmental Protection Agency

TRISTAN BOYER BINNS

Heinemann Library
Chicago, Illinois

Published by Heinemann Library,
an imprint of Reed Educational & Professional Publishing,
Chicago, IL

Customer Service 888-454-2279

Visit our website at www.heinemannlibrary.com

Page Layout by Molly Heron
Photo research by Jessica Clark
Printed and bound in the United States
by Lake Book Manufacturing, Inc.

07 06 05 04 03
10 9 8 7 6 5 4 3 2 1

Library of Congress Cataloging-in-Publication Data

Binns, Tristan Boyer, 1968-
    EPA : Environmental Protection Agency / Tristan Boyer Binns.
        p. cm. -- (Government agencies)
Includes index.
    Summary: An introduction to the Environmental Protection Agency, discussing its nature, structure, and responsibilities.
    ISBN 1-58810-497-4 (HC), 1-58810-981-X (Pbk)
    1. United States. Environmental Protection Agency--Juvenile literature. 2. Environmental law--United States--Juvenile literature.
[1. United States. Environmental Protection Agency. 2. Environmental law. 3. Environmental protection.] I. Title. II. Series.
    KF3775.Z9 B56 2002
    363.7'0973--dc21

                            2001006762

Acknowledgments
Cover Photograph by Tim Wright/Corbis
mask illustration on all pages by Guy Palm; p. 4, 5T, 8B, 11B, 23, 26 Ohio Environmental Protection Agency; p. 5BL AFP/Corbis; p. 5BR Jim Bourg/ReutersPhoto Archive/NewsCom; p. 6T Houghton Mifflin Company; p. 6B Kenneth Garrett/Woodfin Camp/TimePix; p. 7, 8T, 9T Bettmann/Corbis; p. 9B Gary Braasch/Corbis; p. 11T Michael Rieger/FEMA News Photo; p. 14 Ed Young/Corbis; p. 15T Philip James Corwin/Corbis; p. 15BL, 19T Galen Rowell/Corbis; p. 15BR Todd Buchanan/Getty Images/NewsCom; p. 16BL William James Warren/Corbis; p. 16BR Bill Ross/Corbis; p. 17BL, 24 Ted Spiegel/Corbis; p. 17BR Sal DiMarco/TimePix; p. 18 William Waldron/Getty Images/NewsCom; p. 19R Reed Saxon/AP/WideWorld Photos; p. 20T Natalie Fobes/Corbis; p. 20B Mike Segar/Reuters Photo Archive/NewsCom; p. 21 John Fleck; p. 22 Dominion Resources, Inc.; p. 25T Time Magazine/Time Inc./TimePix; p. 25B Vladmir Repik/Reuters Photo Archive/TimePix; p. 27, 28, 29, 30, 31, 38, 39 U.S. Environmental Protection Agency Region III; p. 32 AFP Photo/NOAA/Corbis; p.33 illustration by Stephen Durke; p. 34, 35B U.S. Environmental Protection Agency; p. 35 T Rudi von Briel/Heinemann Library; p. 36, 37 Courtesy of the Subsurface Protection and Remediation Division, Ada, OK, and Kathy Tynsky of Computer Sciences Corporation/U.S. Environmental Protection Agency; p. 40 Sunwise School Program/U.S. Environmental Protection Agency; p. 41L Girl Scouts of Kentuckiana; p. 41R Girl Scouts; p. 42 Larry Dale Gordon/The Image Bank/Getty Images; p. 43B George Hall/Corbis; p. 43T Marilyn "Angel" Wynn/Nativestock

Every effort has been made to contact copyright holders of any material reproduced in this book. Any omissions will be rectified in subsequent printings if notice is given to the publisher.

The author and publisher would like to thank Leanne Nurse, Sue Warner, Robin Danesi, Bill Smith, Stephanie Branche, Larry Teller, Pat Krantz, Matt Justice.

Note to the Reader: Some words are shown in bold, **like this.** You can find out what they mean by looking in the glossary.

Contents

What Does the EPA Do?

Many people living in the United States do not think about the fresh air they breathe, the clean water they drink, and the healthy land they live on. But some Americans do not have a clean **environment** in which to live. Many animals and plants must live in unhealthy places. The United States government has a whole **agency** that works to protect people and the natural world in the United States. The Environmental Protection Agency, or EPA, is this agency.

The EPA gets its job done in several ways. EPA scientists research how to control **pollution**. Workers and special instruments measure pollution levels to make sure pollution is not getting worse. **Policymakers** look at the results of the measuring and the research. Then they set **standards** about pollution and the environment that everyone has to follow. EPA **enforcement** officers make sure the standards and environmental laws are followed.

Leaders of the EPA want all U.S. citizens and companies to help protect the environment. Businesses and citizens pay taxes that pay for most of the cleanups and extra machinery and workers that make **waste** safer. The EPA shares information and helps people learn about the environment and what is being done to help the environment.

The EPA works with most U.S. government agencies in making policies. It helps businesses make decisions about how to build factories or clean up waste. The EPA also works with foreign countries to help make goals that help everyone protect the environment.

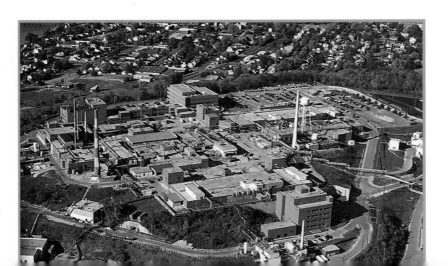

The Mound, in Miamisburg, Ohio, is a nuclear plant being cleaned up with the help of the EPA's **Superfund** Program.

An EPA researcher collects samples to take back to the laboratory for scientific analysis.

A hazardous materials expert with the EPA works to clean up the U.S. Senate office building in Washington, D.C., in November 2001.

A Time of Need

After the September 11, 2001, **terrorist** attacks on the World Trade Center in New York City and the **Pentagon** building near Washington, D.C., EPA workers made sure the air was safe to breathe and the water was safe to drink. Stations with special instruments tested the air near the Pentagon and World Trade Center, looking for dangerous chemicals. Because a dangerous material was found in the air and in the dust near the World Trade Center site, rescue workers had to wear special masks so they could breathe safely. EPA workers built special showers so they could wash the dust off their bodies and clothes when they finished work. Where problems were found in the dust on buildings, cars, and streets, big vacuum trucks swept it up.

Before the EPA

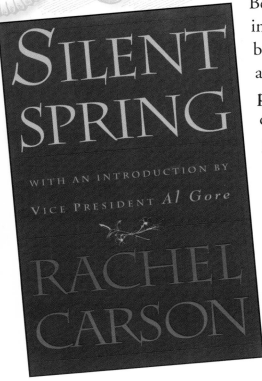

Rachel Carson's *Silent Spring* was originally published in 1962. For this 1994 edition, Al Gore, who was Vice President at the time, wrote the introduction.

Before 1962, many Americans were not interested in **environmental issues**. Then a book called *Silent Spring* was published. The author, Rachel Carson, wrote about how **pesticides** were killing birds. She also described the dangers of pesticides on foods people ate. The book was very popular. Many Americans started thinking carefully about the environment.

During the 1960s, some Americans also worried about how they would survive in such a **polluted** world. Many leaders around the world blamed the United States for most of the environment's problems because the U.S. made and used the largest amount of the world's **resources**.

Also, in 1969, President Richard Nixon wanted the U.S. government to help clean up the environment. He asked politicians and citizens to help him. Then **Congress** passed a law called NEPA, the National Environmental **Policy** Act.

William Ruckelshaus was the first administrator of the Environmental Protection Agency.

A group of women and children in New York works to clean up the city on the first Earth Day, April 22, 1970.

This new law called for the government to help Americans learn about the environment and to fix the damage done to the environment. On April 22, 1970, the first Earth Day was celebrated. Almost 20 million people all over the United States participated.

On December 2, 1970, the EPA was created. Other government **agencies** had been responsibile for different parts of the environment. The EPA took over those responsibilities as well. At first, the EPA had many offices in Washington, D.C. Making a team with many people working in different places was hard. The first administrator of the EPA, William Ruckelshaus, did a great job of giving the EPA an important mission. He started an attack on pollution as soon as the EPA began.

The Early Days

The EPA's first important law was the Clean Air Act of 1970. It set **standards** for air quality. This law put limits on how much **pollution** factories could release into the air. It also set goals for lowering how much car engines could pollute. Each state was allowed to **enforce** the Clean Air Act on its own. EPA workers made sure the states and businesses were following the laws.

In March 1971, many EPA workers moved into a large office building in Washington, D.C. Ten offices across the country also were opened. About 5,000 people worked for the EPA then. Now more than 18,000 people work for the EPA, and it spends more than $7 billion a year.

These protesters are gathered outside the EPA's headquarters in Washington, D.C.

EPA successes include:

- Lowering the amount of lead (a dangerous substance) that children are exposed to by controlling lead-based paint

- Banning DDT, a very harmful **pesticide** that can hurt animals and cause cancer in people

- Stopping dangerous untreated **sewage** from flowing into rivers and lakes

The EPA won its first enforcement battle in 1971 when the Union Carbide Plant in Marietta, Ohio, finally agreed to a plan that would reduce their air-polluting **emissions** by 70 percent.

- Cleaning up the Great Lakes, which were very polluted
- Setting standards for the quality of drinking water
- Making lists of how much **fuel** different types of cars use, so people can see which types of cars use the least
- Controlling **hazardous waste** from when it is made until it is when it is disposed of
- Banning **toxic** chemicals like PCBs, which cause cancer
- Protecting the **ozone layer** by banning CFCs, which were used to make spray cans work and to keep refrigerators cold
- Cleaning up toxic waste sites, such as Love Canal in New York in 1980
- Making businesses tell the people who live near them about the kinds of toxic chemicals they use and what they do to keep people safe from those chemicals
- Fining businesses that break the laws and pollute the **environment**, such as Exxon after its tanker, the *Exxon Valdez*, spilled oil in Alaska in 1989
- Helping government, businesses, and people recycle more waste, including hazardous waste
- Working with businesses to make safer pesticides to replace the older, more dangerous kinds
- Making factories reduce the amount of toxic emissions they put into the air

Many families lived in the Love Canal neighborhood until it was discovered that the community was sitting on top of an old toxic waste dump.

After the *Exxon Valdez* oil spill off the shore of Alaska in 1989, an otter tries to shake off oil stuck to his fur. Many animals died as a result of the oil spill.

At first, the EPA thought all pollution could be controlled or removed by using **technology.** With better ways to clean pollution and the EPA asking for and enforcing tough laws, the environment would get better quickly. But now, EPA leaders know it is not that simple. Pollution and environmental damage are hard to clean up, and sometimes the damage is not fixable. Many plants and animals are now **extinct.** The world's **climate** is changing. The balance between keeping the U.S. economy strong and keeping its land safe is hard to strike.

EPA's National Goals

The EPA's has ten main goals that describe its responsibilities.

1 **Clean Air**   The goal of having safe, healthy air throughout the United States will help people, especially children. As the air is cleaned up in places with dirty air, animals and plants will also be healthier.

2 **Clean and Safe Water**   The goal of clean water will help people, animals, plants, and land. Clean rivers, oceans, and lakes mean wildlife can live there and people can safely play there. Making drinking water safe by managing its sources well also means less flooding.

3 **Safe Food**   The goal of making the food we eat safe from dangerous **pesticides** will help children the most. Children suffer more than adults do from the effects of pesticides.

4 **Preventing Pollution and Reducing Risk**   The goal of having a cleaner and safer **environment** will help everyone. The EPA is working to reduce or remove **emissions** that **pollute** our air, land, and water.

5 **Better Waste Management**   There are two parts to this goal. The first part deals with taking new **wastes** and storing them safely. The second part deals with cleaning up pollution from old waste sites.

6 **Reducing Global Risks**   Working with other countries, the United States will help lower risks from the **ozone layer** shrinking and **climates** changing. The hope is to save **ecosystems** in danger of being hurt or destroyed.

7 **Sharing Information**   EPA leaders believe that people need to know about the environment in the area in which they live. Citizens can work to keep their families safe. People who work with the environment also need to share their findings easily.

8 **Better Science**   New scientific findings can help to protect the environment. Science and research can also help solve the old problems of how to clean up **toxic** wastes.

9 **Enforcing Laws** By making businesses and people follow environmental laws, they can help improve the environment.

10 **Managing Itself Better** The EPA needs to be as well managed as possible to reach its goals and help people and the environment.

This EPA worker is checking an air sampling location set up around the site of the World Trade Center.

Special suits protect EPA workers as they clean up **hazardous** pollution.

The Structure of the EPA

The EPA is divided into ten **regions**, plus a national headquarters in Washington, D.C. The top staff, or leaders who are in charge of the national divisions, work in offices in the headquarters. The overall administrator, who is in charge of the entire EPA, also works there.

Workers in each region are responsible for making sure that EPA programs work within their region. Each region has scientists, researchers, **enforcement** officers, and lawyers. The regional offices can be big, with up to 1,000 **employees**.

Know It

A major part of the EPA's purpose is sharing **environmental** information with the public. The Office of Environmental Information helps collect and organize information. It is often organized into **databases** on computers, then shared through the Internet or published papers.

This map shows the ten regions of the EPA. Each regional office is responsible for carrying out the EPA's programs in its area.

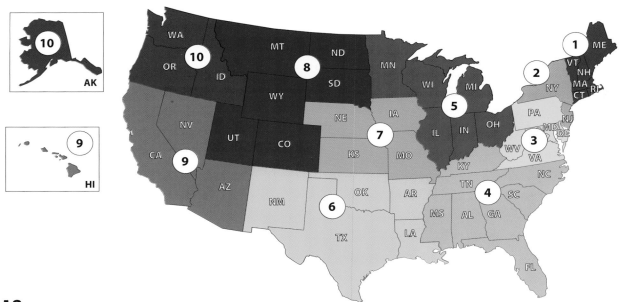

EPA

Organization Structure

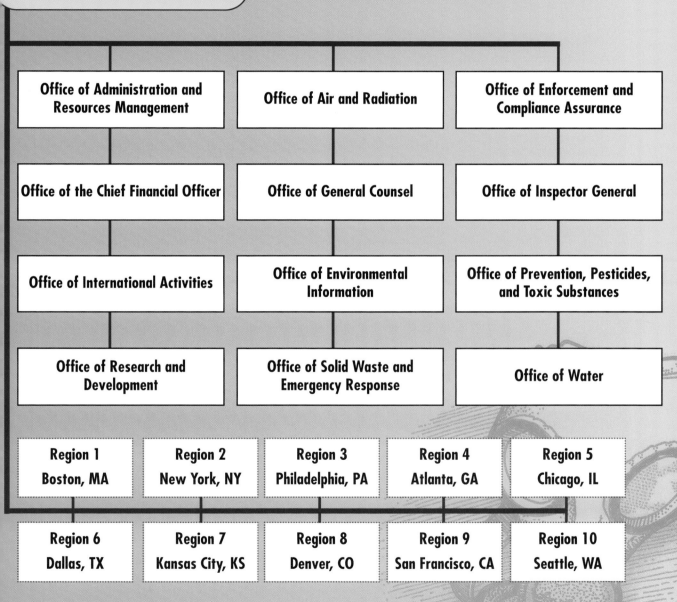

Deputy Administrator

Office of Administration and Resources Management	Office of Air and Radiation	Office of Enforcement and Compliance Assurance
Office of the Chief Financial Officer	Office of General Counsel	Office of Inspector General
Office of International Activities	Office of Environmental Information	Office of Prevention, Pesticides, and Toxic Substances
Office of Research and Development	Office of Solid Waste and Emergency Response	Office of Water

Region 1 Boston, MA	Region 2 New York, NY	Region 3 Philadelphia, PA	Region 4 Atlanta, GA	Region 5 Chicago, IL
Region 6 Dallas, TX	Region 7 Kansas City, KS	Region 8 Denver, CO	Region 9 San Francisco, CA	Region 10 Seattle, WA

All Around Us

One of the ways Americans are put at risk is through dangerous **pesticides** and **toxic** chemicals on their food and in the **environment** around them. The EPA's Office of Prevention, Pesticides, and Toxic Substances works to lower that risk. This office has three divisions.

Workers in the Office of **Pollution** Prevention and Toxics help teach people and businesses how to prevent pollution. If chemicals must be used, EPA workers help people choose the safest ones for the job. They also tell people about the risks of chemicals. Workers in this office also teach people how to safely remove dangerous materials that were used many years earlier, such as asbestos and lead.

A new pesticide must pass many tests before it is approved by the EPA.

Workers in the Office of Pesticide Programs control how pesticides are used, which pesticides are allowed, and who can make and sell them. Before a pesticide is approved, EPA **employees** do more than 100 tests to make sure it won't hurt people or the environment. They also test to see how much is left of the pesticide on food when it is harvested. Anyone who makes or sells pesticides has to be **registered.** Pesticides that have been in use for a long time are reviewed to make sure they follow today's **standards.** People who apply pesticides are taught how to protect themselves from the chemicals. Workers also look for other ways to control pests besides using pesticides, such as using a pest's natural predator to control pest populations on crops.

Workers in the Office of Science Coordination and **Policy** help the other offices with scientific research. Some of the scientists are researching ways to control pests without using pesticides. Others are researching possible health problems from older pesticides.

Some Ways to Stop Pollution

You can help stop pollution. At home, you can make choices that will help lower the amount of carbon dioxide going into the air. Carbon dioxide is one of the gases that cause **global warming.**

These kids are getting rid of their aluminum cans the environmentally sound way—by recycling them.

Doing this: will lower carbon dioxide this much:

- Planting two trees:
  20 lbs (9 kg) a year less
- Buying things with recyclable packaging: 230 lbs (104 kg) a year less
- Recycling everything possible at home: 850 lbs (386 kg) a year less

All of these pesticides contain a very dangerous poison called DDT. They were widely available until the mid-1960s.

This worker wears protective clothing to remove asbestos, a cancer-causing material, from a building. At one time, asbestos was commonly used to insulate buildings.

15

Air Pollution

All living things, from plants to animals to people, need air to survive. If that air is **polluted,** the living things that breathe it will not be as healthy. Pollution comes from many sources. Most air pollution is invisible, but that doesn't mean it is harmless. Air pollution can change **climates,** cause **global warming,** destroy the **ozone layer,** make smog near the ground, cause cancer, and damage plants and water. The EPA's Office of Air and Radiation works to stop air pollution.

Within the Office of Air and Radiation, workers in the Office of Air Quality Planning and **Standards** study air quality. Experts here decide how much of six major pollutants, such as lead and smog, are safe to breathe. They check air all over the United States to make sure it meets the standards. **Employees** make **databases** of information so problems can be studied. These people also write reports and tell politicians and citizens about the air quality where they live.

The Office of Atmospheric Programs looks at problems in the sky, such as acid rain. Acid rain is caused by the **emissions** from factories and **power plants.** Chemicals in the emissions mix with air and fall to the earth as acidic rainwater. Acid rain can kill trees and plants and make water in lakes and rivers poisonous to fish. Employees in the Office of Atmospheric Programs work to lower emissions levels and control the acid rain problem.

Los Angeles has a problem with smog, a type of air pollution that you can see. The picture on the left was taken at dawn on a day when the air quality was good. The picture on the right was taken when the air quality was bad. The smog makes it difficult to see and hard to breathe.

They are also trying to protect the ozone layer by **banning** the chemicals that damage it. These workers are also trying to stop global warming by helping businesses and people understand how to use energy in safer and more efficient ways. Emissions from burning **fuels,** such as gasoline in car engines or coal in power plants, add to global warming. Saving energy by burning fewer fuels will help.

The problem of emissions from engines that burn fuel is so serious that all the workers in the Office of Transportation and Air Quality are trying to solve this problem. They help carmakers build cleaner-burning car engines. They also write the standards for inspections of car emissions.

Americans spend up to nine times more time inside than outside. The air quality inside buildings is as important as the air quality outside. Employees in the Office of Radiation and Indoor Air work to keep indoor pollution down. Household and office machines, such as appliances, photocopiers, and furnaces, can cause indoor pollution.

These plants will be exposed to simulated rains with different levels of emissions so that scientists can study the effects of acid rain.

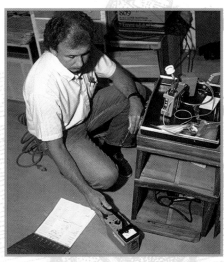

An inspector checks for dangerous radon gas in a basement.

Water Pollution

Most of the earth's surface is covered with water. But the water that people and most animals drink comes from only a tiny part of it. It is important to keep that water clean so people and animals can survive. But it is also necessary to the health of the earth that all water is clean. Even the water that we can't drink, such as saltwater and water frozen in the polar icecaps, helps keep the planet healthy. **Ecosystems** depend on clean water.

Employees in the EPA's Office of Water work with all kinds of water. These workers set **standards** and try to find the best ways to control and stop water **pollution**. These workers also decided who can dump **waste** and how much. They are always working to lower the levels of **bacteria** in water that cause diseases, and also the levels of toxic chemicals in water.

Employees in the Office of Water's Office of Science and **Technology** do a lot of research. Some study what happens when ships dump waste into water. Some make sure that the water along beaches is safe for swimmers. Experts in this office also study the risks of toxic sediment. Sediment is tiny pieces of dirt or sand that move with river water. If sediment moves through toxic waste, it can be contaminated. Then when the sediment settles to the bottom of a river,

Hudson River

In August 2001, the EPA decided to clean **sediment** that was **contaminated** with dangerous **toxic** chemicals from the bottom of the Hudson River in New York. The General Electric company dumped chemicals in the river for more than 35 years before the chemicals were **banned** in 1977. There are about 1.1 million pounds (598,957 kilograms) of toxic chemicals in the river. As they clean the river, workers test the water to make sure they haven't spread the toxic chemicals.

The abandoned Hudson Falls General Electric plant sits on the Hudson River in New York.

An EPA scientist checks arctic waters for signs of contamination.

Signs of water pollution are visible at this beach in Southern California.

animals and fish can eat it, making them toxic as well. Some sediment was contaminated many years ago before there were standards to stop toxic waste dumping. Now contaminated sediment has to be removed by lifting it carefully from the bottom and **disposing** of it properly.

The other three offices within the Office of Water are in charge of managing **wastewater,** wetlands, **watersheds,** ground water, and drinking water. Workers in these offices set and **enforce** standards, and organize cleanups where they are needed. Watersheds are of great concern. A watershed is the area that feeds the source of drinking water for a place. If the watershed is clean, the chances of having clean drinking water are higher. People help by cleaning up watersheds and making sure nothing contaminates the area.

Land Pollution

Land can be **polluted** in many ways. Most of the trash that we throw away is solid **waste**, and it needs to be put somewhere. Most trash is put in places called **landfills**. Everyday, trash in landfills is covered with dirt to keep rats and other pests out. When the landfill cannot hold any more trash, it is covered with more earth and grass is planted on top. Then the area can be used as a sledding hill, a golf course, or for other uses. However, the building and using of landfills needs to be done properly. If a **hazardous** material is dumped in a landfill, it may seep into the **groundwater**. Some waste must be burned to be **disposed** of properly. Even the smoke and ash need to be checked to make sure they are safe.

The EPA's Office of Solid Waste and Emergency Response works on ways to better handle solid waste. Scientists look for ways to use the energy created by landfill sites. As trash in landfills decomposes, or breaks down, it produces gas that might be used as energy. Other scientists teach people how to recycle more trash, buy products with less packaging, and **compost** yard and food waste. When hazardous waste needs to be disposed of, workers in this office help find the best ways to do it. The experts here **regulate** the underground storage tanks used to hold hazardous materials.

Workers clean oil off rocks after the *Exxon Valdez* disaster.

All of the debris from the World Trade Center attacks, including destroyed rescue vehicles and fire trucks, was taken to this landfill on Staten Island.

Accidents can happen, even when people are careful and follow all the rules. Most communities have plans that tell leaders what to do in case of a chemical spill or leak. Experts in the EPA's Office of Solid Waste and Emergency Response help make those plans and decisions about what to do in case of an accident. This office also lets people in communities know about risks near them.

Oil spills can be very dangerous, on land as well as in water. Americans use more than 250 billion gallons (947 billion liters) of petroleum oil each year. Most oil is use to run cars and heat houses. This oil has to be moved from the oil companies to the people who use it, and things can go wrong.

Sometimes old hazardous waste was not disposed of properly. Workers in the Office of Solid Waste and Emergency Response help clean it up. If the people or companies responsible for the problem cannot be found, then a government program called **Superfund** pays for the clean up. More than 50,000 U.S. government sites are also **contaminated** and need to be cleaned up. EPA scientists are always working to make new and better ways to clean up soil and **groundwater**.

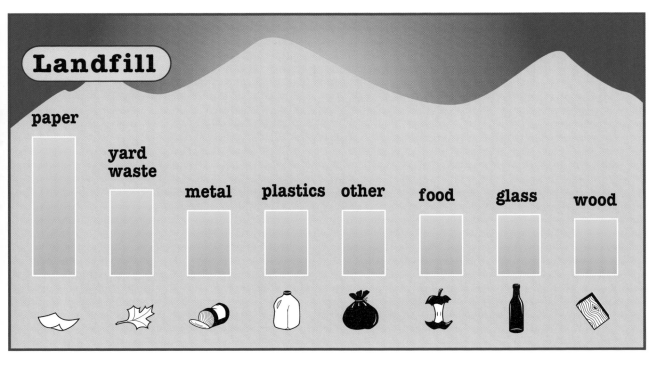

Of all the trash that goes into landfills, paper makes up the biggest share. Recycling material like paper, metal, plastic, and glass reduces the amount of trash dumped into landfills.

A Closer Look: Superfund

In 1980, the United States **Congress** made a powerful law that created the **Superfund** Program to clean up the most **polluted** places in the country. **Hazardous waste** dumping had been going on for many years, often illegally. Thousands of places in the United States needed to be cleaned to protect the people living nearby. Some sites were old **landfills** or warehouses. And in many of these places, **toxic** waste had seeped into the **groundwater,** making many people sick with diseases, such as cancer.

Often, the companies that dumped the hazardous waste will help with the cleanup. But if the site is a hazardous emergency, Superfund does the work first and looks for the responsible people later.

Superfund success: York County, Virginia

Between 1957 and 1974, the local power company, Virginia Power, burned coal and petroleum coke to generate electricity. The fly ash left from the burning was dumped nearby in sand quarries. By 1980, a family nearby reported that their drinking water was turning strange colors. The water had poisonous **heavy metals** in it that had come from the ash in the quarries. Virginia Power worked with the county

The laughter of children can be heard on the fields of Chisman Creek Park, Virginia.

government and the people who lived in the community to clean up the area and the water. A high-tech drainage system and treatment plant was installed, and workers covered the ash with a thick layer of clay. A park with softball diamonds and soccer fields was built on the clay cap. After four years, the water was clean enough to go straight into the drinking water supply without being filtered.

Cleaning up a toxic site can take years. It requires a lot of money as well as time. Scientists have invented new ways to clean places more quickly and inexpensively than before. Many more sites are being cleaned up now than ever before. Since Superfund began in 1980, about 800 sites have been made safe again. However, almost 1,200 more sites are waiting to be cleaned up.

Superfund success: Bowers Landfill, Ohio

During the 1960s, about 7,500 tons (6,806 metric tons) of chemical waste were dumped at this landfill. By 1980, toxic wastes had **contaminated** the water, soil, plants, and animals in the area. People could be hurt by just breathing the air at the site. The top layer of the landfill was removed, then clay was put on top. The water was checked carefully for chemicals. A wetlands area was developed on top of the clay cap, so the site is now safely used by wildlife.

Before and after: How the landfill looked after a flood in 1991 (top), and how it looked after construction was completed in 1999 (bottom).

International Activities

The United States shares the earth with many other countries. And although our laws stop at our borders, the **pollution** we create doesn't. **Toxic** gas clouds made in one country can drift into a neighboring country. Countries sharing rivers, lakes, or other waters also must share what is dumped into the water. Toxic chemicals, especially **pesticides**, may be illegal in one country but legal in another. The EPA works with other countries' governments to protect all citizens.

Officials in the EPA's Office of International Activities work closely with workers in the governments of Canada and Mexico. They make sure **hazardous waste** is carried properly across borders. The United States also shares **ecosystems** with Mexico and Canada. EPA specialists work with Canadian and Mexican specialists to protect these ecosystems from damage from air, water, and land pollution. Together, these workers try to protect forests or other habitats threatened by pollution and save animals and plants that are near **extinction**.

The Office of International Activities also works with many foreign countries on the **issues** of **global warming** and **climate** change. When countries agree to create less pollution, everyone can benefit. For example, since 1987, countries have worked together to greatly lower the amount of

Representatives from the EPA attend an international conference in Germany about controlling air pollution.

materials used around the world that harm the **ozone layer.** EPA workers have become leaders in this fight by teaching specialists in foreign countries how to make and use energy in cleaner ways.

Part of the responsibility of working with other countries to protect the global **environment** means sharing **technology.** Where the EPA can help, workers create programs to teach people how to gather and share information about the environment. They also teach people skills so they can create their own programs to help the environment.

Environmental Disaster

An example of an very bad accident that caused many problems is the Chernobyl nuclear **power plant** explosion in the former Soviet Union. On April 25, 1986, the power station blew up, sending **radioactive** material high into the air. Carried by the wind, this cloud traveled far. It left radioactive material around the Chernobyl site, but also in many other European countries. The radioactive cloud dumped the deadly material on trees and plants. Some people who worked with the **contaminated** trees and plants got sick. Forest foods, like mushrooms, were also very contaminated. Contaminated lakes and rivers are still a problem. It may take up to 100 years to find out how badly **groundwater** has been contaminated by the Chernobyl accident. All of the countries that were under this radioactive cloud are working together to solve the environmental problems the Chernobyl disaster caused.

The Chernobyl disaster in the former Soviet Union spread radioactive material through many European countries, contaminating water, plants, and wildlife.

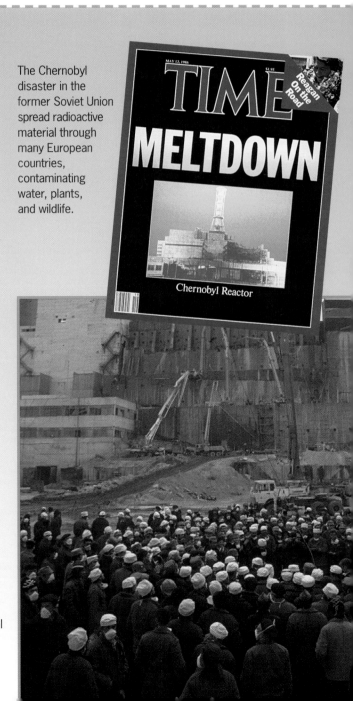

Chernobyl Reactor

After the Chernobyl reactor exploded, teams worked quickly to seal it up to prevent even more dangerous material from spreading.

The Workers

There are many different jobs at the EPA. It takes many kinds of skills to protect the **environment**. The EPA needs specialists to test for pollutants, scientists to discover new ways to reduce **pollution**, and communications specialists to share information with the citizens. Workers who help the specialists are also important.

Most environmental **policy** is written at headquarters in Washington, D.C. For example, lawyers and scientists who work at the EPA headquarters usually help write the EPA's new rules and **regulations.** EPA workers in the ten **regions** help to **enforce** the rules.

Special Jobs at the EPA

Environmental Scientists can be specialists in almost any kind of science. Some help investigate problems, and others perform tests on water, air, and soil. Some scientists work outside laboratories, helping to write new rules or to teach others.

Environmental Engineers develop and help people understand new ways to stop pollution or clean it up.

Environmental Protection Specialists work to reduce pollution and clean up the environment.

A day in the outdoors can be quite busy for an EPA scientist. Samples can be taken from the soil, plants, animals, and water that are found in the area.

Field **Investigators** inspect companies that have permission to dump small amounts of pollution. The investigators make sure the companies follow the laws. Field investigators also check places where they think there might be a problem. They take samples to try to find out who is responsible for the pollution.

Criminal **Investigators** handle cases where pollution is a crime. Most EPA rules are not criminal laws, but sometimes the polluter acts in a criminal manner and should be punished.

Public Relations and Environmental Education workers communicate with newspapers, television reporters, schools, and the public. They are responsible for making sure that Americans know how to help the environment, what the laws are, and who has broken them. Many other EPA employees work with schools, talking about their jobs or running exercises in how to reach agreements.

Special Agent Jack Adudell is in charge of the EPA's Region 3 office in Philadelphia.

Roy Seneca is a press officer for the Region 3 office.

A Closer Look: Working for the Cities

Stephanie Branche always knew she wanted to help protect the **environment**. She studied environmental science in college and spent time as an **intern** at EPA headquarters in Washington, D.C. In her first job at the EPA in Philadelphia, Pennsylvania, she helped write rules about underground **fuel** storage tanks and chemical spills.

Stephanie also worked with the Congressional and State Liaison Officer for Virginia. This means she worked with politicians and environmental groups in the state of Virginia. Because she knew a lot about science, she was able to explain why certain environmental rules were important.

Stephanie Branche works hard to prevent urban sprawl by making cities better places to live.

Now Stephanie is working on a new project. It is called Urban Smart Growth. In many places across the United States, cities are growing so much that empty land must be used for new homes, businesses, and roads. This kind of growth without thorough planning is called sprawl. Urban Smart Growth was created by a group of seventeen federal **agencies** including the EPA.

Stephanie takes a water sample from the Schuylkill River in Philadelphia.

In her job, Stephanie is working to make three cities in her area better places to live, so people do not want to move away. This helps to stop sprawl. A big part of the program is developing unused parts of cities. There are many places in cities where **toxic** chemicals were dumped. EPA workers are working to clean these places and put new businesses on the sites. Stephanie is also working to develop the waterfront of the Delaware and Schuylkill Rivers in Philadelphia.

Stephanie works on location to clean up a **contaminated** site in Philadelphia so that it can be redeveloped.

Workers in Urban Smart Growth also work with local citizens. College researchers help think of good ways to protect the environment. Stephanie is working to help more people live near where they work so they can walk or ride bikes to and from their jobs instead of driving cars. Also, many cars can be changed so they run on new fuels that **pollute** less. Unfortunately, most cities don't have any gas stations that sell this new fuel. Stephanie is working to change this.

A Closer Look: EPA Lawyer

EPA Lawyer Bill Smith works at his office.

Two kinds of lawyers work for the EPA. **Enforcement** lawyers work to stop **polluters** from breaking U.S. **environmental** laws. **Regulatory** lawyers work in **regional** offices, giving advice about the EPA's rules, or regulations, that protect air, water, and land.

Bill Smith has been a lawyer with the EPA for ten years. He has always worked at the EPA's Region III office in Philadelphia, Pennsylvania. For the first five years, he worked as an enforcement lawyer on the Clean Air Act. When a field inspector discovered a company that was breaking the Clean Air Act, Bill helped get the company to follow the law. First he would send them a notice that they had broken the law. Then he would talk with the company and its lawyers about the problem. A complaint would be filed by the EPA. The company had to give answers to the complaint. EPA lawyers and the company's lawyers would have more talks and share information with each other. Finally, both sides would reach an agreement, called a settlement. However, some problems would have to be decided by a judge.

Now Bill works as a regulatory lawyer on Clean Water Act **permits.** EPA officials know that some pollution cannot be avoided. Factories, farms, construction sites, and **sewage treatment plants** all create pollution. But these places are very necessary. To control the amount of pollution these

Bill discusses Clean Water Act permits during a meeting.

places make, the EPA works with states to give permits that say what kinds of pollution and how much are allowed.

Bill spends most of his day answering questions, having meetings about legal problems, and reading permits that the EPA is about to grant. All the lawyers in his office who work on the Clean Water Act get together frequently to discuss their cases and changes in the law. They often ask each other questions about new cases and help each other learn as much as they can to do their jobs well. Bill enjoys his job because when he does it well, it means he's doing good for both the public and the environment.

Bill's job is satisfying because he knows the work he does will help the environment.

Scientific Advances

Fires in Western United States
01:15 UTC 22 August 2000
GOES-8 RGB = CH 1,2,4

MONTANA

WASHINGTON

smoke

PACIFIC OCEAN

OREGON

WYOMING

IDAHO

NEVADA

EPA scientists can collect data on the environment by looking at satellite pictures like this. The yellow in this picture shows forest fires burning in Idaho and Montana.

Without scientific research, EPA officials would not be able to set **standards** about how much **pollution** is harmful to the **environment** and people. They would not discover new ways to control pollution. They would not find ways to **dispose** of old pollutants. The Office of Research and Development is very valuable to the EPA, because workers here do most of the EPA's research.

Workers in this office check the environment to make sure that new pollution problems are discovered. They try to predict environmental problems and think of ways to stop the problems from happening. One way EPA scientists do this is by looking at information collected from satellites orbiting the earth.

When beginning their research, EPA scientists follow a set of steps. They want to see how big the risk of having an environmental or human problem is. They then want to figure out how to handle the risk so it is as low as possible. Scientists keep talking with each other, learning from the work they are doing. They are always looking to see if another scientist's research can help their own research. Here are the steps EPA scientists follow:

1. Find out what kind of problem it is and how big it is.

2. Find out how people or the environment were exposed to the chemical or whatever substance is causing the problem.

3. Decide how big the risk of having the problem is, based on the information from the first two steps.

4. Find ways to end exposure to the cause of the problem, or make the cause less dangerous.

Research has helped lower risks in a number of ways. For instance, scientists have learned better ways to tell if drinking water is **contaminated.** Lead is often a necessary material used when building a house. But lead can make people sick. EPA researchers have learned how to make homes with lead safer for children to live in. By teaching people how to control the lead, fewer children will get sick.

CAT Scans

One way to know how healthy a body of water is is to count how many animals are living in the ground beneath the water. Scientists take a sample of the ground and then count the animals, but the counting can take a long time. Scientists now use CAT scans of the ground samples to make their job easier. CAT scans are like very good X rays. Animals living in ground beneath water make tunnels, like ants do. Healthy ground has many tunnels. The CAT scan shows clearly how many tunnels there are, so the scientists can count the tunnels quickly and accurately.

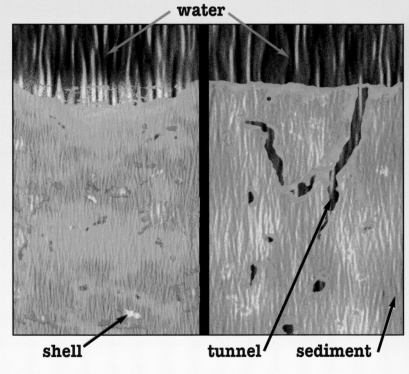

In this CAT scan of a **sediment** sample, blue indicates water, and green, red, and orange are sediment. Yellow represents shells.

The EPA's Laboratories

The EPA has laboratories all across the United States. The scientists in these labs work on research projects to help the EPA discover **environmental** damage and learn ways to fix it.

The National Health and Environmental Effects Research Laboratory has seven locations. The most important laboratory is at the Research Triangle Park in North Carolina, the EPA's largest research site. This laboratory researches how **pollution** harms people and the environment. The other locations do other kinds of research. For example, the Gulf Ecology Division in Florida researches pollution and what it does to Florida's bodies of water.

The EPA's largest research site is located in the Research Triangle Park in North Carolina. The EPA office in Research Triangle Park focuses on three major functions: administration and management, regulations, and research and development.

The National Exposure Research Laboratory is at the Research Triangle Park. This lab helps find out what might happen because of a new chemical or environmental change, such as changing the flow of a river. Researchers here try to predict how changes in **climate** will affect the earth. Researchers at the National Risk Management Research Laboratory in Cincinnati, Ohio, study ways to make pollution less dangerous. All of this research helps EPA officials know about the dangers of pollution and environmental changes.

Researchers in the National **Vehicle** and **Fuel Emissions** Laboratory test engines, vehicles, and **fuels** to see how much they pollute. They develop new ways to control emissions, using science and **technology**. Workers here also make sure that companies that make vehicles follow the **standards** for emissions and do not make vehicles that use too much gasoline. They also help create the standards and programs that require vehicles that pollute even less.

The National Risk Management Research Laboratory is part of the EPA's office of Research and Development.

Thirsty Trees Fight Pollution

Researchers at the at the National Risk Management Research Laboratory are studying how trees can help clean polluted soil and **groundwater.** Trees planted on polluted soil pull water and chemicals up into their roots. The trees soak up the **toxic** chemicals, but they still grow well! Planting trees might be a good way to help clean up some of the 40,000 **hazardous waste** sites across the United States.

A Closer Look: Robert S. Kerr Environmental Research Laboratory

Scientists at the Kerr Center come up with new ways to clean polluted groundwater.

Each of the EPA's laboratories specializes in one part of **environmental** science. The Robert S. Kerr Environmental Research Laboratory in Ada, Oklahoma, works on **groundwater** research. Scientists here research how groundwater is affected by **pollution**. They also develop new ways to clean it up.

Because groundwater can be deep underground, it often is difficult to test and clean. Workers in this laboratory use special drills to pull out ground samples for testing. The drills can dig new water wells to test how chemicals might clean polluted groundwater.

The Kerr Center has 37 specialized laboratories. Researchers use many different kinds of scientific equipment to do their research. Some equipment tells what chemicals are present in samples. Other equipment helps separate materials in samples. The Kerr Center also has special places to store the chemicals it uses and the **hazardous waste** it produces.

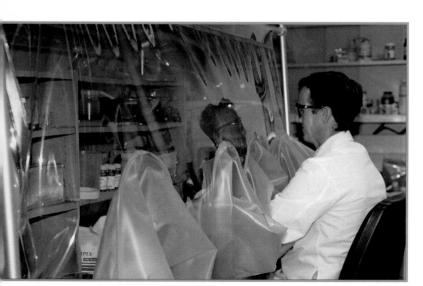

Scientists try to re-create the original environment of **sediment** samples in order to study them accurately.

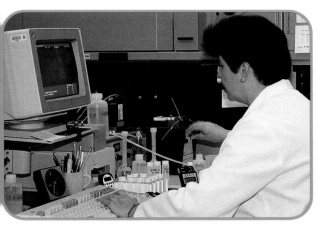

An analytical chemist performs metal analysis.

This scientist is testing materials to determine their radioactivity levels.

Many different kinds of scientists work at the laboratory. Chemists, biologists, geologists, physicists, and soil scientists all work here. Mathematicians and computer specialists also work at the Kerr Center. Working together, the scientists have developed new ways of getting samples for testing. They have also created a very successful way to clean up **contaminated** groundwater using **bacteria** that eat the pollution! The laboratory's scientists often work with scientists throughout the United States and around the world. They share information and try to solve difficult environmental problems.

One of the Kerr Center's successful projects helped farmers better **dispose** of the waste their animals produced. Another helped oil companies treat land damaged by the **byproducts** of making oil. Researchers at the Kerr Center keep working to learn new ways to treat pollution underground. Using heat, vacuuming up soil, using soap to wash out pollutants, and putting up special barriers are methods being studied now.

Researchers at the Kerr Center work with scientists all over the world to solve difficult environmental problems.

A Closer Look: EPA Chemist

Every day that Sue Warner goes to work is an interesting challenge. She works for the EPA in Region III's lab on Fort Meade Army Base in Maryland. Sue is a chemist. She has worked for the EPA for more than fourteen years. Doing chemistry for the EPA is like detective work. Sue receives a sample of water, soil, or **waste** without knowing much about it. These samples are made up of different chemicals. Each has a chemical "fingerprint" that tells it apart from other chemicals. Sue uses an instrument called a gas chronometer to separate the sample into its different chemicals. Then she uses a computer to tell what the chemicals are and how much are in the sample. With Sue's help, **hazardous** chemicals in the samples can be found and identified.

Sue works with other scientists who also test for different kinds of chemicals. They also look for **pesticides** and **heavy metals.** These tests show how acidic samples are and if they have **sewage** in them. Some workers count how many small animals, such as

Sue works with students to teach them about the kind of chemistry she does at her job.

Students are often amazed at how many items they use everyday are actually causing **pollution.**

worms, live in a body of water. They can tell how healthy the water is by how many animals live in it. All of this information is put into reports. Sue reads her coworkers' reports to make sure the methods used and information given make sense.

Sue also has other responsibilities. She does inspections of other labs that do tests for the EPA. She gives tours to visitors and helps train foreign scientists and other EPA workers. Sue enjoys going to local schools and working with students. She has taught classes and judged science fairs. She has also brought a mobile lab out and done experiments with the students. Sue enjoys all the different parts of her job, but loves helping solve environmental problems most of all.

The mobile lab travels all around to different schools, bringing hands-on science education to elementary students.

The EPA Reaching Out

Some EPA **employees** work with businesses and communities on special projects that protect the **environment.** This program is called Project XL— "XL" stands for "excellence and leadership." EPA officials and community leaders think that many people working together can help develop new ways to solve air **pollution** and **waste** management problems.

Know It

In 1972, the Cuyahoga River in Ohio caught fire because it was so polluted! Today almost half of all rivers and lakes still do not meet EPA water quality standards.

The SunWise School Program is an EPA program put together to help teachers and students learn about sun protection. Students learn what sunshine is and how the **ozone layer** protects the earth. Most students study outside, learning how to protect themselves from the sun. Without protection, the risks of eye damage and skin cancer are much higher.

The Girl Scouts of the U.S.A. are working with the EPA to help clean up **watersheds.** Girl Scouts can earn a Water Drop patch by learning about water pollution. They can help by learning how water is used in their homes

Students in the SunWise School Program perform experiments to learn about the ozone layer and sunshine.

and then thinking of ways to use less water and make less pollution. Many scouts walk along rivers and lakes in their communities and describe what they see. Some visit **sewage treatment plants** to learn how **wastewater** is treated to become safe again. Girl Scouts visit aquariums to learn how plants and animals use water to survive. After learning about water pollution, Girl Scouts make art projects, write poetry, or construct displays about water pollution. They can also teach younger children what they have learned. By the time they earn the Water Drop patch, the scouts know how to make a difference in protecting their community's water **resources**.

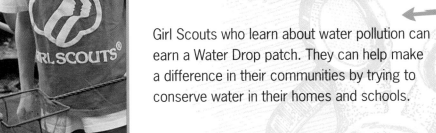

Girl Scouts who learn about water pollution can earn a Water Drop patch. They can help make a difference in their communities by trying to conserve water in their homes and schools.

The Future of the EPA

EPA officials would like every American's goal to be a cleaner **environment**. They want the thousands of EPA **employees** working together with companies and communities to help protect the environment. If everyone can agree on how to protect the environment, the environment will be the winner. In the past, the EPA had to punish people and companies for breaking environmental laws. Now, the EPA is also giving awards for environmental successes.

It is impossible for EPA workers to know about every company that **pollutes** the environment. Some companies are now helping the EPA by studying how clean their factories are and how much pollution they create. When company leaders find a problem, they can ask the EPA for help. EPA workers can help decide how to fix the problem. The more companies that work like this, the better job the EPA will be able to do.

Mercury is a dangerous chemical often used in making thermometers. The EPA is working with the American Hospital Association to get mercury out of all hospitals.

Sometimes companies help the environment by sharing research. Chemical companies work with the EPA to create lists of information that describe chemicals. Because more people are working on the project, the information can be gathered and used sooner to help protect people and the environment.

The EPA also wants people in companies and communities to have access to environmental information. By making information easy to reach on a web site, the EPA has given people tools to work well at home to protect the environment. People can see where danger areas are and get facts about the environment.

Living on the Land

Native Americans use the environment as part of their everyday life, from religious rituals to growing food. Because many Native Americans live very closely with the land, they can be hurt badly when the environment is polluted. The EPA works with Native Americans in different tribes to share information and clean up the environment.

The traditional Native American lifestyle is closely tied to nature. The EPA is working with Native Americans to help keep their land clean and healthy.

The EPA helps companies like airlines find ways to lessen the pollution they produce.

Further Reading

Baird, Nicola. *A Green World?* Danbury, Conn.: Franklin Watts, 1998.

Beals, Kevin, and Carolyn Willard. *Environmental Detectives.* Berkeley, Calif.: University of California, Berkeley, Lawrence Hall of Science, 2001.

Byrnes, Patricia. *Environmental Pioneers.* Minneapolis: Oliver Press, Inc., 1998.

Chapman, Matthew and Rob Bowden. *Air Pollution: Our Impact on the Planet.* Austin, Tex.: Raintree Steck-Vaughn Publishers, 2002.

Harmon, Daniel. *The Environmental Protection Agency.* Broomall, Penn.: Chelsea House Publishers, 2003.

Hunter, Rebecca M. *Pollution and Conservation.* Austin, Tex.: Raintree Steck-Vaughn Publishers, 2001.

Jackson, Donna. *The Wildlife Detectives: How Scientists Fight Crimes Against Nature.* New York: Houghton Mifflin, 2000.

Kidd, J. S. and Renee A. *Into Thin Air: The Problem of Air Pollution.* New York: Facts on File, 1998.

Maze, Stephanie. *I Want to Be an Environmentalist.* New York: Harcourt Children's Books, 2000.

National Wildlife Federation Staff. *Pollution: Problems and Solutions.* Broomall, Penn.: Chelsea House Publishers, 1999.

Taylor, Barbara. *How to Save the Planet.* Danbury, Conn.: Franklin Watts, 2001.

Thompson, Gail. *Kids Care for the Earth.* Washington, D.C.: National Geographic Society, 2002.

Contacting the EPA

Environmental Protection Agency
Ariel Rios Building
1200 Pennsylvania Avenue, N.W.
Washington, D.C. 20460
(202) 260-2090

Region 1 (CT, MA, ME, NH, RI, VT)
Environmental Protection Agency
1 Congress St. Suite 1100
Boston, MA 02114-2023
http://www.epa.gov/region01/
Phone: (617) 918-1111
Fax: (617) 565-3660
Toll free within Region 1: (888) 372-7341

Region 2 (NJ, NY, PR, VI)
Environmental Protection Agency
290 Broadway
New York, NY 10007-1866
http://www.epa.gov/region02/
Phone: (212) 637-3000
Fax: (212) 637-3526

Region 3 (DC, DE, MD, PA, VA, WV)
Environmental Protection Agency
1650 Arch Street
Philadelphia, PA 19103-2029
http://www.epa.gov/region03/
Phone: (215) 814-5000
Fax: (215) 814-5103
Toll free: (800) 438-2474
Email: r3public@epa.gov

Region 4 (AL, FL, GA, KY, MS, NC, SC, TN)
Environmental Protection Agency
Atlanta Federal Center
61 Forsyth Street, SW
Atlanta, GA 30303-3104
http://www.epa.gov/region04/
Phone: (404) 562-9900
Fax: (404) 562-8174
Toll free: (800) 241-1754

Region 5 (IL, IN, MI, MN, OH, WI)
Environmental Protection Agency
77 West Jackson Boulevard
Chicago, IL 60604-3507
http://www.epa.gov/region5/
Phone: (312) 353-2000
Fax: (312) 353-4135
Toll free within Region 5: (800) 621-8431

Region 6 (AR, LA, NM, OK, TX)
Environmental Protection Agency
Fountain Place 12th Floor, Suite 1200
1445 Ross Avenue
Dallas, TX 75202-2733
http://www.epa.gov/region06/
Phone: (214) 665-2200
Fax: (214) 665-7113
Toll free within Region 6: (800) 887-6063

Region 7 (IA, KS, MO, NE)
Environmental Protection Agency
901 North 5th Street
Kansas City, KS 66101
http://www.epa.gov/region07/
Phone: (913) 551-7003
Toll free: (800) 223-0425

Region 8 (CO, MT, ND, SD, UT, WY)
Environmental Protection Agency
999 18th Street Suite 500
Denver, CO 80202-2466
http://www.epa.gov/region08/
Phone: (303) 312-6312
Fax: (303) 312-6339
Toll free: (800) 227-8917
Email: r8eisc@epa.gov

Region 9 (AZ, CA, HI, NV)
Environmental Protection Agency
75 Hawthorne Street
San Francisco, CA 94105
http://www.epa.gov/region09/
Phone: (415) 744-1305
Fax: (415) 744-2499
Email: r9.info@epa.gov

Region 10 (AK, ID, OR, WA)
Environmental Protection Agency
1200 Sixth Avenue
Seattle, WA 98101
http://www.epa.gov/region10/
Phone: (206) 553-1200
Fax: (206) 553-0149
Toll free: (800) 424-4372

Glossary

agency   part of a government responsible for a certain task

analyzing   to study something complex by breaking it down into its smaller parts

bacteria   tiny creatures that live in water, soil, or animals and may cause disease

ban   to stop use of

byproduct   unwanted thing that is produced as a result of a process

climate   the way the weather works in a part of the world

compost   to gather organic waste, such as yard clippings and vegetable matter, in a pile so it can naturally break down into material called compost that is good for the soil

Congress   main lawmaking group in the United States, made up of separate houses of senators and respresentatives

contaminated   made dangerous by mixing with hazardous materials

database   system that stores information in such a way that it can be used easily, usually on a computer

dispose   to get rid of

ecosystem   community of plants, animals, and environment

emissions   materials sent into the air, water, or soil

employee   worker for a company or organization

enforce   to carry out

environment   climate, soil, water, air, and the living things in a place

extinct   when the last one of an entire kind of plant or animal dies, that kind is extinct and cannot come back

fuel   what powers an engine—usually a form of oil

global warming   when the temperatures around the world are rising, making the whole world warmer

groundwater   water that is stored inside the earth that feeds wells and springs for drinking water

hazardous   very dangerous

heavy metals   metals that are dangerous to people and animals, like lead and mercury

intern   someone who works at a company or organization for a short period of time to gain experience

investigator   someone who looks into something very deeply

issues   ideas or rules that people take sides on

landfill   area where garbage is buried between layers of earth

ozone layer   part of the atmosphere surrounding the earth that keeps dangerous rays from the sun out and heat in

Pentagon   headquarters of the U.S. Department of Defense

permit   written document that gives the holder permission to do something

pesticide   chemicals that kill insects and other pests on crops

policy   accepted way of doing something. Someone who helps decide what is done about something, or how something is thought of is called a policymaker.

pollute   to make soil, water, or air dirty with smoke or chemicals or other waste. A pollutant is something that causes pollution.

power plant   big factory where electrical power is made

radioactive   when something is contaminated by dangerous chemicals called radiation

registered   to get official permission to do something

region   area that is part of a larger area

regulate   to make rules for the production and use of

resources   things that are used to make other things, or that are important to survival, like drinking water

sediment   matter that sinks to the bottom of a liquid, such as a body of water

sewage   waste from people and animals, both liquid and solid

sewage treatment plants   places where sewage is separated into waste to be thrown out and clean water

solvent   chemical that dissolves things

standard   guideline or rule

Superfund   EPA program that helps clean up major pollution sites

technology   the use of science in the wider world

terrorism   using or threatening violence in order to influence a government

toxic   very dangerous to living things

vehicle   any kind of machine that transports things or people, usually using an engine

waste   garbage or trash that no one wants anymore

wastewater   water that has been used and is dirty, often resulting from a manufacturing process

watershed   area that feeds the source of drinking water for a place

Index